CATS DOMINO

DOGSBODIES

A BOOK OF CANINE NONSENSE
DRAWINGS AND VERSES
BY SIMON DREW

dog daze

ANTIQUE COLLECTORS' CLUB

dedicated to
plug
nutty meg crack trip peach
toots molly lady joss indy
goldie lister jenny biddy
harley michaela trigger
maisie louis snip mipsie
pip moss bryth pepsi pimms
max factor herbie
dd sammy
sally monday custard

and
caroline

holier than thou

©1997 Simon Drew
Reprinted 2008
World copyright reserved

ISBN 978-1-85149-271-8

British Library Cataloguing-in-Publication Data
A catalogue record for this book is available from the
British Library

Printed in China
for the Antique Collectors' Club Ltd., Woodbridge, Suffolk

A BLESSING IN DISGUISE

A NEW BREED

I had a dream that I would soon fulfill,
to breed a dog that answered to my will.
I needed genes from bloodlines clean and pure,
untainted strains of which I could be sure.
And all my best endeavours soon bore fruit:
a tiny puppy – bright and soft and cute.

O come O come Emmanuel
For I've just bred a King Charles Spaniel.

guide dogs for the obese

fig 1:   how to play bridge

fig 2:   how to play contract bridge

fig 3:   a bridge too far

a dog-eared page

9

a dog is for life
not just for christmas dinner

compulsory
crumpet
balancing

crumpet
voluntary

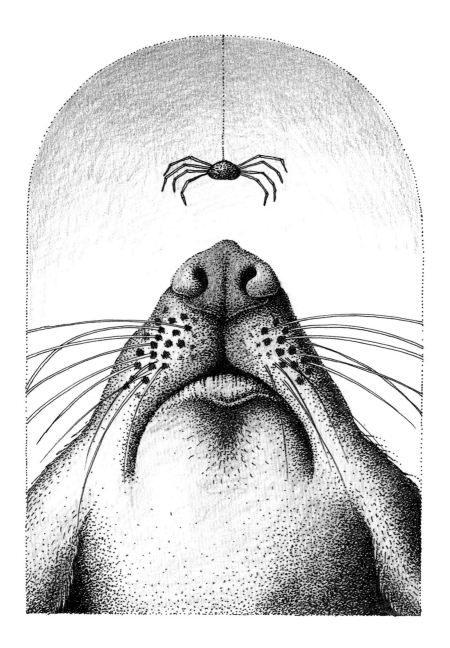

SPIDER·WITH·ROSIE

A HAPPY ENDING

Behold the jolly jailbird –
he's happy with his fate.
Tomorrow they release him –
he's just one day to wait.
His sentence will be over:
he's past his cell-by date.

BASIC TRAINING

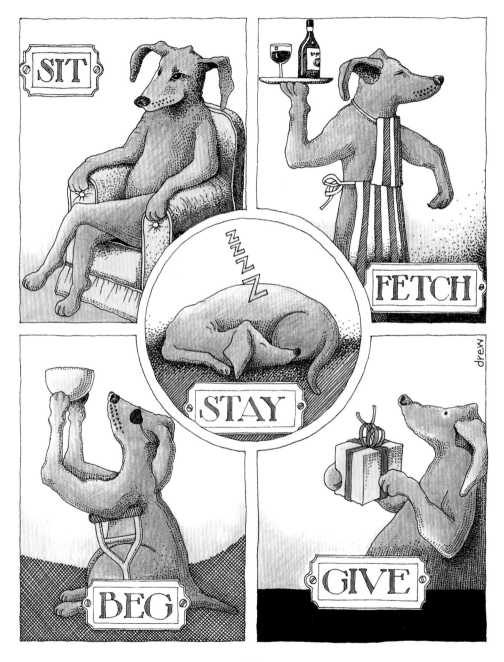

ADVANCED TRAINING

There aint nothing like a Dane

tails of the riverbank

PHILOSOPHER

Please join the line and form a Q
Philosopher will answer U
                    (quite soon)
Please come and ask the reason Y
And he will close a thoughtful I
                    (but not for long)
And while he's brewing cups of T,
Elucidate, and you will C
                    (from his answer):
'Our life is like a flying J,
whose summer's spent in making A
                    (while the sun shines).

THREE DOGS
MAKING 'A'
(WHILE THE SUN SHINES)

drew

dog on a dual cabbage way

drew

BOB AND THE HYENAS

This is a comparison
between Bob,
an Italian air traffic controller,
and the hyena,
a most unfortunate coarse wild dog
that lives in the dark corners
of Africa.

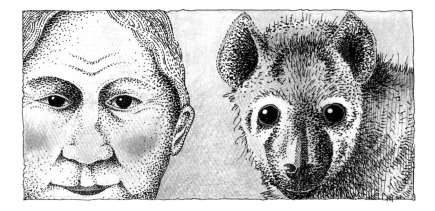

Just one of them eats chicken with his
                              hands
and neither do they share a common home.
Hyenas roam the plains of foreign lands
and Bob lands all the foreign
                         planes in Rome.

an old sea dog

an old can't-see dog

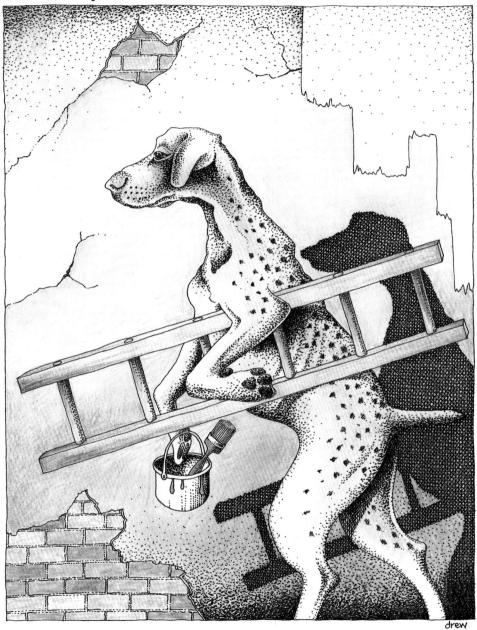

Pointer and Decorator

great mistakes of history:

rossing the alps with 2 aardvarks and a whippet

the twelve labels of Hercules

Hell and Dalmatian

SUPERSTITION

The wind was blowing cold
like a snort from an eskimo's nose.
The owl was hooting loud
in the day (which is odd, I suppose).
The chap with ice cream treats
was a man with a mission to sell
but how could anyone buy
from a man with no stories to tell?

Somewhere something moved:
how could that noise have occurred?
Was it a flapping bat
or the squawk from a colourful bird?
Or was it a croaking frog
or a whispering chatter of bears?
No: you must listen hard:
it was superdog saying his prayers.

Never teach an old dog newt tricks

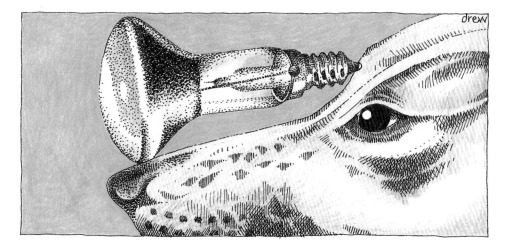

How many dogs does it take to change
a light bulb?
Would it be 3?
Would it be 33?
Standing on each others backs.
Growling and whining.
Would it be 45?
Straining to reach the socket.
Would it be 52?
With one barking out instructions.
Or maybe 79?
With one section singing encouraging songs
and others forming a pyramid of cheerleaders.
Could it be 96?
Formed into 8 groups of 12 with each
group taking a shift in turn.

But from their task they'll never shirk
for many hounds will make light work.

WHISTLER'S MONGREL

the last of the mohicans' dog

SEMAPHORE EXPLAINED

cleanliness is next to dogliness

While inspecting ladders
in a french handyman shop

Am I nailed down to the floor?
Although I've not been here before
I'm sure I'd like to move away
or am I here for ever?

Leaden shoes; so weighted down;
they feel so huge; am I a clown?
I cannot move: I start to pray.
(I'm feeling not so clever).

Glistening floors: I think it's glue.
I've lost the bottom of my shoe:
I may be here a little time
whatever my endeavour.

Adhesive fools have spilt a tin.
I hope it doesn't reach my skin
(and if this verse is going to rhyme
I think their name is Trevor).

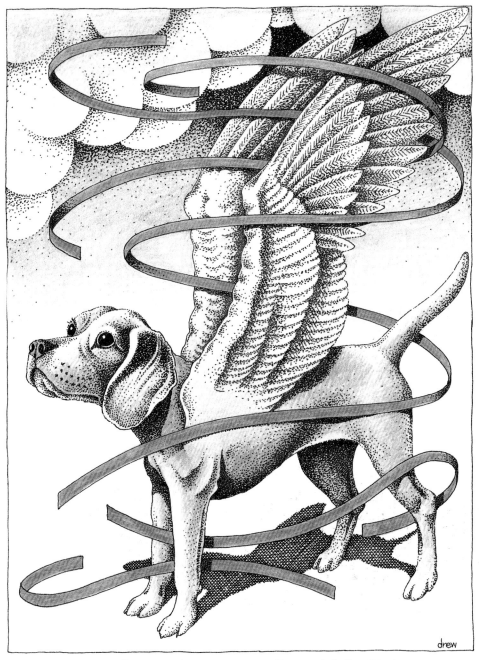

THE BEAGLE HAS LANDED

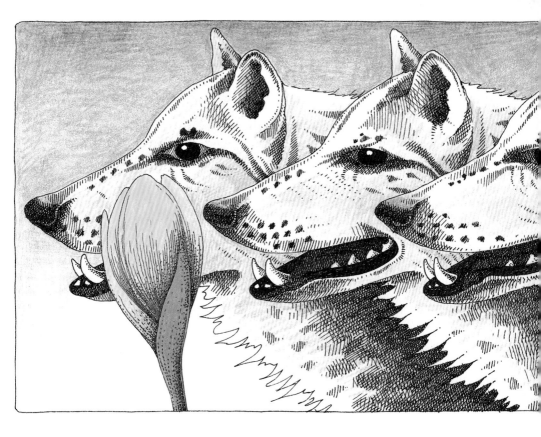

INNOCENCE

She wandered through the hollihocks,
meandered past the wishing well,
and jumped the roses by the rocks
while all about her growled the dogs of hell.

She watched the tadpoles swimming by
in oxbow lakes along the dell;
the beauty of it made her sigh
while all about her barked the dogs of hell.

The fragrant scent of tulips here
would burst upon her sense of smell
for she was deaf and couldn't hear
that all about her howled the hounds of hell.

OUR MESSAGE TO THE NATION
"Ascot week
is our favourite occasion.
We love to see chaps in their fresh morning dress
and girls in their bonnets make such an invasion."
This is the lifestyle of Corgi and Bess.

"Polo match
on the back lawn tomorrow.
It's the horses I like here, I have to confess:
presenting the trophies will fill me with sorrow."
This is the lifestyle of Corgi and Bess.

"Sandringham,
and the living is easy,
(although we must hide from the men of the press).
We take out the dogs when it's sunny and breezy."
This is the lifestyle of Corgi and Bess.

"Christmastime
and we don't know who's coming;
family life is a little like chess
and still the old house doesn't cope with the
                                        plumbing."
This is the lifestyle of Corgi and Bess.

"But, you know,
that I feel like a loser;
the hymn's about me when it's saying God Bless
but nobody let's me drink pints at the boozer.
Call this a lifestyle. God save me," said Bess.

Corgi and Bess

the old believe everything:
the middle-aged suspect everything:
the young know everything.

oscar wilde

'I sometimes think that God,
in creating man,
somewhat overestimated his ability.'

oscar wilde

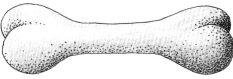

'To win back my youth, there is nothing I
wouldn't do — except take exercise,
get up early or be a useful member
of the community.'   Oscar Wilde

'when people agree with me
I always feel that I must be wrong.'
(oscar wilde)

only dull people
are bright at breakfast.